THE MOTHER GOOSE
COOKIE-CANDY BOOK

by Anne Rockwell

Random House 🏠 New York

Copyright © 1983 by Anne Rockwell. All rights reserved under International and Pan-American Copyright Conventions. Published in the United States by Random House, Inc., New York, and simultaneously in Canada by Random House of Canada Limited, Toronto. *Library of Congress Cataloging in Publication Data:* Rockwell, Anne F. The Mother Goose cookie-candy book. SUMMARY: A collection of recipes for cookies, cakes, and candies with a nursery theme including Peter Rabbit's Carrot Bars, Humpty Dumpty's Peanut Brittle, and the Queen of Hearts' Jam Tarts. 1. Cookies—Juvenile literature. 2. Candy—Juvenile literature. [1. Cookies. 2. Candy. 3. Cake. 4. Cookery] I. Title. TX772.R63 1983 641.8'654 82-13268 ISBN: 0-394-85500-0 (trade); 0-394-95500-5 (lib. bdg.) Manufactured in the United States of America 1 2 3 4 5 6 7 8 9 0

A NOTE TO PARENTS

The desserts that follow are ones children love to eat. Sharing in their preparation is a wonderful (and delicious) family experience. The drawings are meant to be helpful as well as decorative, for they illustrate the directions step by step.

Though the recipes are simplified so even the most novice adult cook can make them, none is intended to be made by a child alone. And each parent, knowing his own child, must take responsibility for choosing which steps are suitable to his young helper's skill.

An adult should always light the stove, light the oven, and remove hot pans from them; but children can safely mix, stir, cream, measure, sift, beat eggs, grease pans, roll dough, cut out, ice, and decorate cookies with minimal adult supervision.

The extra-hot sugar mixtures needed for the candy recipes can be dangerous for children, so these recipes should be made by an adult unassisted. But children can help gather ingredients, measure, pour, and grease platters—not to mention carry out the most gratifying steps in those recipes such as shaping and wrapping popcorn balls; stretching and cracking peanut brittle; and pulling, cutting, and wrapping taffy.

All the ingredients in this book are readily available. When eggs are called for, large eggs are intended. When butter is called for, salt butter is meant—it's easier to find and much cheaper. You can substitute margarine for butter if you wish, but there will be a considerable flavor loss in jam tarts and sugar cookies. Be sure to always use pure vanilla extract instead of artificial vanilla flavoring. And level all dry ingredients when measuring them.

Certain terms appear repeatedly in the recipes and are basic cooking techniques. *Creaming* consists of rubbing butter up against the sides of a mixing bowl with the back of a wooden spoon until the butter becomes soft and fluffy. Then sugar is added, very gradually, and blended

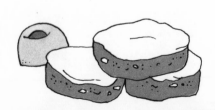

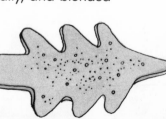

into the butter. When a recipe says to *beat* with a wooden spoon, it means you should turn the mixture over forcefully with the spoon, adding air to the batter as you do so. You will hear a plopping sound as you beat. *Stirring* or *mixing* simply means to stir around and around with a wooden spoon until the dry ingredients are thoroughly mixed with the wet, without necessarily adding air to the batter, as in beating.

Though it is possible to use an electric mixer, food processor, or blender for some of the steps, I have avoided mentioning them since children can safely use a wooden spoon, egg beater, or hand grater (with supervision) to do anything an electrical appliance can do.

It's helpful to have a candy thermometer for the candy recipes, but not essential. If you do use one, follow the manufacturer's directions. Many thermometers will break if inserted into a liquid that is already hot.

Although you can roll out dough on a clean kitchen counter or tabletop, you will find a wooden pastry board very helpful. Avoid using a chopping block on which vegetables have been cut, or your cookies may have a hint of onion or garlic.

Rolled cookies, like sugar cookies and gingerbread men, are easier to roll and cut when the dough is cold. Cold dough does not stick as readily to the rolling pin or the pastry board. The technique of lifting a cut-out cookie from the pastry board to the cookie sheet is not difficult for adults, but children may need some tactfully offered help. Put the leavings of dough back in the refrigerator to cool until you are ready to roll out and cut more cookies.

You can add a tasty dimension to your Christmas tree by turning the cookies in this book into ornaments. To do that, first open paper clips so they form an S shape. Space the raw cookies far from one another on the cookie sheet. Then press each paper clip down flat so the smaller part of the S is hidden in a cookie and the larger part of the S is lying on the cookie sheet. Use care when removing the baked cookie decorations from the sheet—the metal clips will be hot. After the cookies have cooled, hang them from your tree. Naturally, just the cookies without clip hangers are meant for eating.

Whether you display these treats as decorations or pop them into willing mouths, they're fun to make with your child. Happy cooking!

GINGERBREAD MEN

1. Put ¼ cup softened butter in a large mixing bowl. Cream the butter with the back of a wooden spoon. Gradually add ½ cup granulated sugar and cream the butter and sugar together until the mixture is light and fluffy.

2. Add ¾ cup molasses. Stir the butter, sugar, and molasses together well.

3. Grate fine ½ teaspoon lemon rind. Add this to the butter, sugar, and molasses.

4. Sift together 4 cups flour, 1 teaspoon baking soda, ½ teaspoon cinnamon, 2 teaspoons ginger, ¼ teaspoon nutmeg, and ½ teaspoon salt.

5. Add half the dry ingredients to the molasses mixture. Stir them together with a wooden spoon. Add ⅓ cup water. Mix with the wooden spoon.

6. Add the rest of the dry ingredients. Flour your hands and then mix everything together with your hands. Add 2 tablespoons of water if the mixture doesn't stick together.

7. Grease 2 cookie sheets with vegetable shortening.

8. Preheat the oven to 350°F.

9. Dust a wooden pastry board or clean countertop with flour. Dust a rolling pin with flour. Roll out the dough evenly.

10. Cut out gingerbread men with a gingerbread man cutter. Lift the gingerbread men onto the cookie sheets with a spatula.

11. Decorate the gingerbread men with raisins and cut-up candied cherries. If you wish to use them for Christmas ornaments, put a paper clip through the heads as shown before the gingerbread men are baked.

12. Bake the gingerbread men 12 to 15 minutes, until they are lightly browned around the edges. Remove them carefully with a spatula from the cookie sheets and let them cool on wire cake racks. Makes about 3 dozen.

1. Sift together into a large mixing bowl 1½ cups flour, ½ teaspoon baking soda, ½ teaspoon salt, 1 cup granulated sugar, and ½ teaspoon cinnamon.

2. Melt ½ cup butter in a saucepan over low heat. Once the butter has melted, take the pot off the fire.

3. Preheat the oven to 350°F.

4. Beat one egg with an egg beater. Add ¼ cup milk, ½ cup vegetable oil, the melted butter, and 1 tablespoon molasses to the egg.

5. Add the egg and milk mixture to the flour mixture. Stir well.

6. Stir in ½ cup raisins, ½ cup broken walnut meats, and then 1¾ cups uncooked oatmeal (regular or quick-cooking, but not instant).

OATMEAL COOKIES

7. Drop the batter, one teaspoonful at a time, onto ungreased cookie sheets and bake 9 to 12 minutes until the edges are brown.

8. Remove the cookies with a spatula. Let them cool on wire cake racks. Makes about 3 dozen.

1. Preheat the oven to 375°F.

2. Grease 2 cookie sheets with vegetable shortening.

3. Put 1 cup softened butter in a large mixing bowl. Cream the butter with the back of a wooden spoon.

4. Gradually add 1 cup granulated sugar and cream the butter and sugar together. Then gradually add 1 cup brown sugar and cream the mixture until it is light and fluffy.

5. Add 2 eggs, beating the mixture with the wooden spoon.

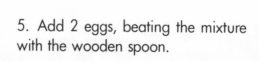

6. Beat in 1 teaspoon vanilla extract.

CHOCOLATE CHIP COOKIES

7. Sift together 2½ cups flour, ½ teaspoon salt, and 1 teaspoon baking soda.

8. Gradually stir the flour mixture into the butter mixture.

9. Stir in 1 cup chocolate chips and 1 cup broken walnut or pecan meats.

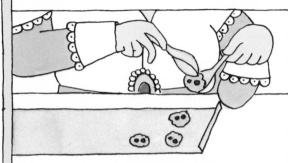

10. Drop the cookie batter from a teaspoon onto the greased cookie sheets. Space the cookies out well, for they will spread as they bake.

11. Bake for 10 to 12 minutes. Remove them from the cookie sheets with a spatula onto wire cake racks to cool. Makes about 3 dozen.

1. Put ½ cup softened butter in a large mixing bowl. Cream the butter with the back of a wooden spoon.

2. Gradually add ⅔ cup granulated sugar and cream the butter and sugar together until the mixture is light and fluffy.

3. Add 1 egg, then beat well with a wooden spoon. Do the same with another egg. Beat in 1 teaspoon vanilla extract.

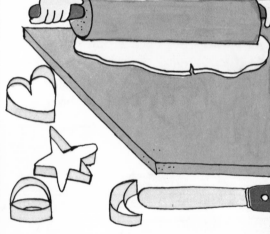

4. Sift together 2½ cups flour with 2 teaspoons baking powder.
   Stir the flour mixture into the butter mixture. Mix well.

5. Cover the bowl with plastic wrap and put it in the refrigerator. Chill the dough for at least an hour. Preheat oven to 350°F. Grease 2 cookie sheets with vegetable shortening.

6. Roll out the chilled dough, a small amount at a time, onto a lightly floured pastry board or clean countertop. Cut into shapes with a cookie cutter. Leave in the refrigerator any dough you are not rolling.

SUGAR COOKIES

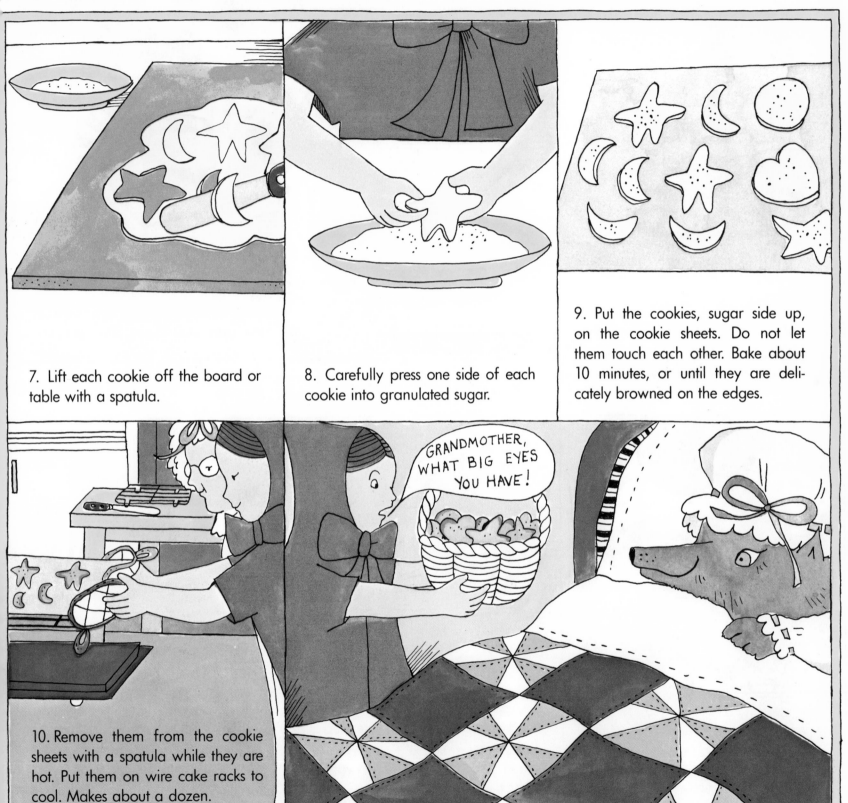

7. Lift each cookie off the board or table with a spatula.

8. Carefully press one side of each cookie into granulated sugar.

9. Put the cookies, sugar side up, on the cookie sheets. Do not let them touch each other. Bake about 10 minutes, or until they are delicately browned on the edges.

10. Remove them from the cookie sheets with a spatula while they are hot. Put them on wire cake racks to cool. Makes about a dozen.

GRANDMOTHER, WHAT BIG EYES YOU HAVE!

—THE THREE BEARS' BROWNIES—

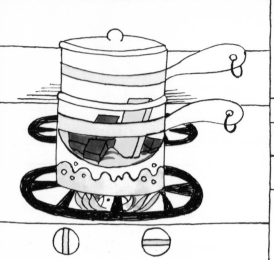

1. Melt ½ cup butter and 4 ounces or squares of unsweetened chocolate in a double boiler. Let the mixture cool.

2. Preheat the oven to 350°F.

3. Grease a 9- x 13-inch cake pan. Then dust the bottom and sides of the pan with flour. Pour out any excess flour. There should be a light dusting of flour over the inside of the pan.

4. Beat 4 eggs with an egg beater until they are lemon-colored.

5. Add 2 cups granulated sugar to the beaten eggs. Beat the sugar and eggs well with a wooden spoon. Add 1½ teaspoons vanilla extract.

6. Stir the butter and melted chocolate mixture into the sugar and egg mixture.

7. Gradually stir 1 cup flour into the chocolate and egg mixture.

8. Stir in 1 cup broken walnut meats.

9. Pour the batter into the greased and floured cake pan.

10. Bake 25 to 30 minutes, or until a toothpick stuck into the brownies comes out clean.

11. Cut into 1½-inch squares when cool.

12. Remove the brownie squares from the cake pan with a spatula. If you store them in a plastic container, they will stay moist and chewy. Makes about 3 dozen.

1. Put ½ cup softened butter in a large mixing bowl. Cream the butter with the back of a wooden spoon.

2. Gradually add ¾ cup granulated sugar and cream the butter and sugar together until the mixture is light and fluffy.

3. Add 1 egg, then beat well with a wooden spoon. Do the same with another egg. Beat in 1 teaspoon vanilla extract and 1 teaspoon lemon juice.

4. Sift together 1¾ cups flour, 1 teaspoon baking powder, and ¼ teaspoon baking soda.

5. Stir the flour mixture into the butter mixture. Mix well. Chill for at least ½ hour in the refrigerator.

6. Preheat the oven to 350°F. Grease 2 cookie sheets with vegetable shortening.

JAM TARTS

7. Pinch off small pieces of the chilled dough. Shape them with your hands into 1-inch balls. If dough gets too sticky to handle, dust your hands with flour.

8. Put the balls on the cookie sheets about 2 inches apart. Make a hole in the center of each ball with your thumb.

9. Fill each hole carefully with a little bit of jam or jelly. Bake 15 minutes.

10. Lift the cookies from the cookie sheet with a spatula. Let them cool on wire cake racks. Makes 2 to 3 dozen.

PETER RABBIT'S CARROT BARS

1. Grate about 10 large carrots to make 3 cups of grated carrots. Set aside in a bowl.

2. Beat 4 eggs with an egg beater in a large mixing bowl until they are lemon-colored and fluffy. Gradually add 2 cups granulated sugar, beating the sugar into the beaten eggs with a wooden spoon.

3. Sift together 2¼ cups flour, 1 teaspoon baking soda, 1½ teaspoons baking powder, 2 teaspoons cinnamon, and ¾ teaspoon salt.

4. Add half the sifted ingredients to the egg and sugar mixture. Then stir in 1½ cups vegetable oil (not olive oil). Add the rest of the sifted ingredients. Mix well.

5. Stir in the grated carrots, 1½ cups packaged shredded coconut, and 1½ cups broken walnut meats.

6. Preheat the oven to 350°F. Grease two 9- x 13-inch cake pans. Then dust the bottom and sides of the pans with flour. Pour out any excess flour. There should be a light dusting of flour over the inside of the pans.

7. Divide the batter equally between the two pans. Spread it out well so the pan bottoms are covered. Bake 30 to 35 minutes.

8. Make an icing by mixing together a 3-ounce package of cream cheese, 2½ cups confectioner's sugar, 3 tablespoons milk, and 1 teaspoon vanilla extract. Mix well with a wooden spoon and then beat hard with the spoon or an egg beater or electric mixer.

9. Using a rubber spatula, spread the icing over the carrot cakes while they are still warm in the pans. Let them cool in the pans.

10. When cool, cut into 2-inch squares. Remove them carefully with a spatula.

1. Mix 1 cup packaged shredded coconut with ¼ cup water in a small mixing bowl. Let it stand. Open a can of crushed pineapple and into another small bowl pour out 1 cup, with some of its syrup.

2. Put ½ cup softened butter in a large mixing bowl. Cream the butter with the back of a wooden spoon until it is fluffy, then gradually cream in 1 cup granulated sugar.

3. Add 1 egg to the butter and sugar mixture, then beat well with a wooden spoon. Beat in another egg. Add 1 teaspoon vanilla extract.

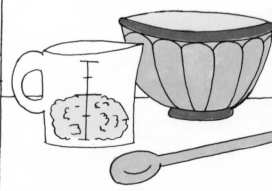

4. Sift together 2½ cups flour, 3 teaspoons baking powder, and ¼ teaspoon salt into another bowl.

5. Stir half the sifted ingredients into the butter, sugar, and egg mixture.

6. Stir half the coconut and water and half the pineapple into the flour, butter, egg, and sugar mixture, stirring well. Add the rest of the sifted ingredients, stirring well.

CUPCAKES

7. Add the rest of the coconut and pineapple, stirring well. Preheat the oven to 375°F.

8. Put paper muffin cups into 3 or 4 muffin tins with spaces for a total of 18 to 24 muffins.

9. Spoon the batter into the muffin cups until they are half full.

10. Bake for 25 to 30 minutes, or until golden brown on top. While the cupcakes are still warm, dust them lightly with confectioner's sugar through a small strainer.

WHO WILL HELP US EAT THESE DELICIOUS CUPCAKES?

I WILL!

I WILL!

I WILL!

I WILL!

1. Measure out ⅔ cup unpopped corn. Put 2 tablespoons cooking oil (not olive oil) in a 4- or 6-quart saucepan with a handle and well-fitting lid.

2. Heat the oil over a medium flame. Drop in two kernels of popcorn. When they jump around very rapidly, the oil is hot enough to add the rest of the popcorn. Put the popcorn in the pan and cover it.

3. Holding the cover with one hand and the handle with the other, shake the popcorn around as it cooks. You will hear it begin to pop.

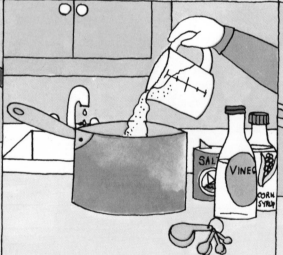

4. After the popcorn stops popping fast, peek inside the cover and see if the pan is full of popped corn. Once it is, remove the pan from the fire and pour the popcorn out into a large heat-proof bowl. Take out any kernels that have not popped. Add ¼ teaspoon salt and mix well.

5. Make syrup by putting 1 cup granulated sugar, ½ cup water, 3 tablespoons white corn syrup, ¼ teaspoon salt, and ½ teaspoon white vinegar in a heavy saucepan that holds at least 2 quarts.

6. Attach a candy thermometer to the side of the pan. Put the pan on medium heat. Stir until the sugar is dissolved. Then stop stirring.

POPCORN BALLS

7. Let the syrup boil up. If sugar crystals form on the sides of the pan, scrape them down with a wooden spoon or a wet pastry brush.

8. Boil without stirring until the syrup reaches 290°F. on the candy thermometer, or until the syrup forms threads that are hard, but not brittle, when dripped from a spoon into a cup of cold water. A very hard ball should form in the water. Remove syrup from the fire and add 1 teaspoon vanilla extract.

9. Pour the syrup over the popcorn. Stir the popcorn and syrup together with the wooden spoon until the two are well mixed.

10. When the popcorn is cool enough to handle, but still warm, smear your hands with butter. Then shape the popcorn into balls.

11. You can wrap the balls with clear plastic wrap and tie each one with a ribbon. They can then be hung on a Christmas tree.

1. Grease a cookie sheet heavily with butter.

2. Put 1 cup granulated sugar, ¼ cup water, and ⅓ cup white corn syrup in a heavy saucepan that holds at least 2 quarts.

3. Measure out 1 cup (about 4 ounces) salted peanuts. Set aside.

4. Attach a candy thermometer to the pan. Put the pan on the stove over medium heat. Stir until the sugar is dissolved, then stop stirring. Let the sugar mixture boil up.

5. As soon as the sugar mixture starts to boil, stir in 2 tablespoons butter. If sugar crystals form on the sides of the pan, scrape them down with a wooden spoon or a wet pastry brush.

6. Cook the syrup, without stirring, over medium heat, until it reaches 300° to 310°F. on the candy thermometer, or until the syrup forms long, brittle threads that crack when the syrup is dripped from a spoon into a cup of cold water.

PEANUT BRITTLE

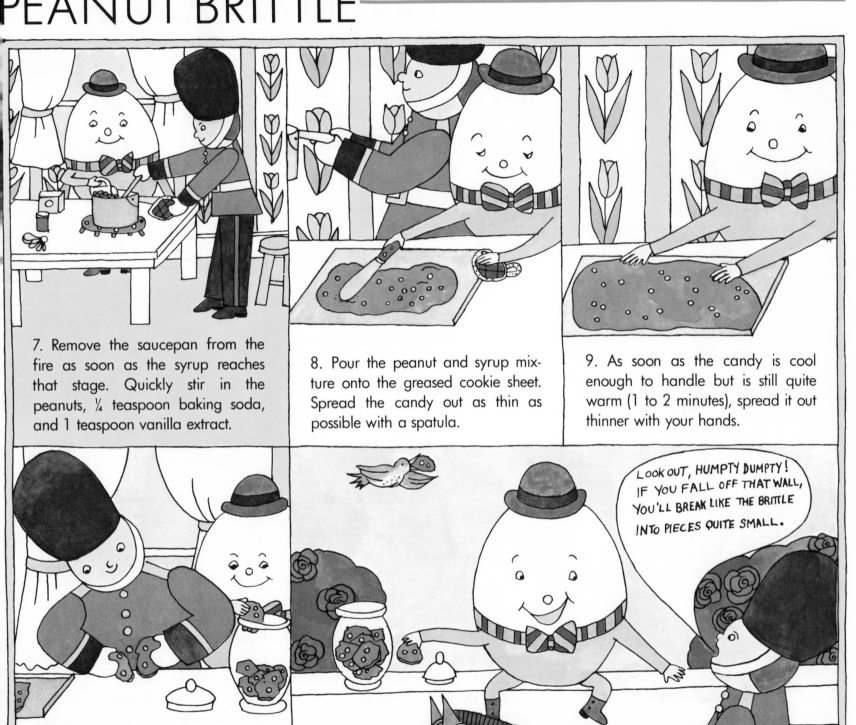

7. Remove the saucepan from the fire as soon as the syrup reaches that stage. Quickly stir in the peanuts, ¼ teaspoon baking soda, and 1 teaspoon vanilla extract.

8. Pour the peanut and syrup mixture onto the greased cookie sheet. Spread the candy out as thin as possible with a spatula.

9. As soon as the candy is cool enough to handle but is still quite warm (1 to 2 minutes), spread it out thinner with your hands.

10. When the peanut brittle is hard and cool, break it into pieces. Store the pieces in an airtight container or it will get sticky from the moisture in the air. Makes about 1½ pounds.

1. Grease a large china platter or cookie sheet with vegetable shortening.

2. Put ½ cup light molasses, 1½ cups granulated sugar, ½ cup white corn syrup, 2 tablespoons white vinegar, ⅔ cup water, and ½ teaspoon salt into a heavy saucepan with high sides. Do not fill the saucepan more than half full. The pot should hold at least 2½ quarts.

3. Attach a candy thermometer to the saucepan, then place the pan on a low fire and stir the syrup with a wooden spoon until the sugar is dissolved. Then stop stirring.

4. Let the syrup boil up over medium heat. If sugar crystals form on the sides of the pan, scrape them down with a wooden spoon or a wet pastry brush.

5. Cook without stirring over medium heat until the candy thermometer reads 220°F. Then add 2 tablespoons butter to the syrup. Continue to cook without stirring over medium to low heat until the thermometer reads 260°F., or until the syrup forms long threads when dripped from a spoon into a cup of cold water and a very firm ball that holds its shape in the water.

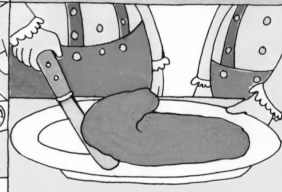

6. Remove the pan from the fire. Pour the syrup carefully onto the greased platter or cookie sheet. Do not stir it or scrape the pan. As the batch of syrup spreads out and becomes solid, fold it over in half with a spatula. Pick it up with the spatula and move it to a cooler spot on the platter. Do this several times, folding it each time you move it.

7. When it is cool enough so you don't burn your fingers, but still warm and soft, grease your hands with vegetable shortening and pick up the taffy and pull it into a rope 2 or 3 feet long.

8. Fold the rope in half.

9. Twist the folded rope around and around.

10. Pull the rope again until it is 2 or 3 feet long. Repeat this pulling, folding, and twisting for 5 to 10 minutes until the taffy is opaque and light-colored. When the taffy begins to harden, pull the rope as long as you can.

11. While one person holds the rope of taffy, another person should grease the blades of a clean pair of scissors and cut the taffy into 1-inch pieces. Wrap each piece in plastic wrap or aluminum foil. Makes about 5 dozen pieces.